# This Is Not For You.

Brittney Jackson

Presentation by *BookLeaf Publishing*

Web: www.bookleafpub.com

E-mail: info@bookleafpub.com

ISBN: 9789395026888

First edition 2022

A Letter To All Of My Exes,


This letter will never reach you.

It was never intended to.

I don't know whether you actually loved me or not, but it doesn't matter to me anymore.

I've forgiven, but I will never forget.

I will never forget the times you made me feel alive.

I will never forget the way you made me want to die.

It fostered me to grow into the adult I am today.

It helped me to realize I needed to work on myself, for myself.

However, I am grateful that you facilitated fixing me overall.

Waves of heartache still come and go, they always will.

So thank you for breaking me,

Making me no longer believe in magic.

Just because we are no longer together does not mean I've changed from a hopeless romantic.

# ACKNOWLEDGEMENT

If I had been okay,
I wouldn't be where I am today.

If I was so convincing,
Why couldn't I convince myself earlier?

You shouldn't have believed me,
You shouldn't have let me self-destruct.
I don't blame you.

You should have fought harder
When I grew angrier.
You should have pulled me in closer
When I pulled away.

I'm so sorry that I broke you into pieces.
I should have let you love me,
You and You
& You...

# PREFACE

This is
Just for you.

Consider yourself
Lucky
I'm wasting words
On you.

Predictable,
Unreliable,
Apathetic fool.

To give up on me
Without reason.

You hide your life away,
I shake my head
Side to side.

Better believe it true--

You're no better
Than me
and I'm no better
Than you.

# Flotsam

Papers
s h r e d d e d

and Ripped to
p i e c e s.

Bonfires light the sky,

My words burning to ashes;

I am forgotten, forever.

All of my words, what a waste…

Watch as they float away,

And disappear into the night.

Ashes to words,

My words to ashes,

Is this what I've been

R e d u c e d

to?

# Oops

She said, "Oops."

Like it was something so miniscule that it
slipped her mind the second after it was sent.
All the while --
It's been eating me alive from the inside,
Minute by dragging minute.
I woke up an hour after I received it,
Kicking myself for not waking up to that
indistinguishable ring I so rarely hear anymore.
The sound that used to be the soundtrack for
almost 360 days of my life.
It's been at the back of my mind for days.
This rusty hopefulness of a true love returning to
me.
Saying --
Finally…
You are good enough for my love.
I know that I am good enough on my own, but I
thought I had found my life partner, my best
friend.
A piece of myself inside of someone else.

So, finally--
I get the nerve to reach out and get that response
to my,

"Did you text me?"
Her: "Oops."

It feels like a scab is being ripped slowly from
my flesh,
My wounds are torn open yet again.
"Oops."

It feels like my nose, it burns, and my eyes well
up with tears.
I've fallen in love once before,
She punched me in the face.
This time, by just one word you uttered (wrote) -
I was punched again.
This time, it somehow felt even worse.

"Oops."
You say you're still not ready to talk to me yet.

My chest feels again,
Like it's exploding.
Re-ploding?
The already existing shards of my heart are
splintering my insides.
I'm bleeding from the old wounds of which I
cannot repair.
I sit in silence,
Nauseated with a pool of blood wading in my
belly.

"Oops."
You say it'll mess up our vibrations.

My hope has all but vanished.
We used to be on the same vibration.
The best I'll ever get again now is only your
friendship,
If I'm lucky - at that.
You'll never love me that hard again.
I had gotten so lucky with you,
I got exactly what I wanted
And then I sabotaged it all.

"Oops."
You say, "Sorry for the confusion."

I have destroyed myself. I understand that
change is a part of life and that no one owes you
a second chance.

"Oops."
You say, you weren't in the right mindset when
you texted me.

Nothing means anything anymore.
I used to balance you.
Our perfect true romance is left in shambles
and I am drowning in regret.

Our cute little family is now a broken home.
I'm unable to reconstruct the splinters of our
infatuation,
The scattered memories of getting lost in each
others' eyes,
Lost forever together -- in another dimension.
Everything has changed...
I've been begging for months for a second
chance at just a conversation,
Nothing.

"Oops."

# Warmest Regards

Sometimes goodbye is

Fluorescent lighting;
Harsh and Stark,
Poignant in all the wrong ways.

Sometimes the hug is brief,
Though the thought of it makes you cry.

Your shoulders are stiff and your face is as hard
as stone,
But the heart feels, and the heart remembers.

There is always time for deep conversation,
Most times there are other things to be done.

Like me,
She does not hold back in written word.

But her presence remains cold.

Some love is silent,
And not sturdy enough to hold.

# Fissure

Night was all around us,
We were walking through
The usual destructions
In our epic story;
And I looked at you,
And knew.

So grave was your expression,
And you no longer held my hand.
We were walking side by side,
But there were whole oceans
and moons and solar systems
Creating a dividing line.
How had such a chasm
Been dug out between us?

I had no answer to that question,
But I knew that your heart
Was no longer with me.

I watched the changing pain,
The shadows of indecision
Passing over your well-loved face;
And how you struggled
With your many transgressions,

Would you be brave enough
To see it for what it was?
You held on to the ideal
We had once built with our hands,
But I knew that it was the
Lingering hold of guilt,
Rather than love.

I could not stop myself
From picking at the scabs,
From chipping at the armor,
From dismantling my dreams,

Brick by
C r u m b l i n g
Brick.

And you took your leave,
Much sooner than I would have
Ever imagined;
Seeing you had been offered
An avenue free of guilt.

But I suffer,
I suffer with your gift,
The gift of love you once offered
And have now retracted
With the gift of love unrequited
That now veils my eyes.

You have condemned me forever
To never feel love, to never feel pain
Without you.
Because it's all tied to you.

Although your absence is merely extra space;
So much of me resided in that space.

In that moment,
When we walked in the darkness,
I knew that it was over,
That you had flown from me
and that you were traveling
So far away,
So far away from
What we had always been.

# Decimation Proclamation

You never write me anything
I've put pen to page
And hand to keyboard
A thousand times over the years;

I find  poetry in my day,
I pour out the stories in my day,
I pour out the stories in my heart.

I stain my hands with ink

And will soon grow arthritic
For the countless words
I've written you,

Even when the ink rubs off onto my clothes
And my hands ache from wrist to fingertip,
I keep writing.

So many letters I've written you;
Letters, words, paragraphs, pages,
Volumes, I've filled only for you.

People sometimes find those words compelling,
Or beautiful,
Or eloquently melancholic.

I'd like to read your words sometime,
Because all I know of them
Are what falls

From
The
Point
Of
My
Pen.

# Curtains

I watched a star fall out of the sky last night,
Right into my hands.

She said only a couple of words to me,
And then she went away.

I started to run after her,
Picking up speed.

I didn't see the light at first,
But as I ran, it grew,
It grew, and it grew, and it grew.

Until it was brighter than the sun.
Until it was bigger than the sea.

I reached for it -- to hold it once again,
For a moment or two was all it seemed.

But when I did, it fell away,
Never to be seen.

It was silent for a second.

Then a scream was heard,

And the scream was lost.

It all seemed to happen so fast.

But then again,


Maybe I just died.

# Brainsick Lunatic

It's amazing how everything you've worked for,
Everything you've spent all of your time
building,
Can amount to nothing

- But -
Empty spaces,
Empty hearts,
Empty places.

It's funny how you can have everything
You've ever wanted,

Watch it all slip away.

Sometimes you think you're in control,
You think you know.
But what do you know?

Nothing.

Nothing but riddles
And pages

Of broken promises
And broken hearts.

Nothing but deceit and betrayal
And tears on tissues you'll never see again.

Watching your dreams
Fall from a 19th story window;
It begins and ends
Right here.

Forgiveness is not an option.

No one understands the words
I scribble onto my notepads.

They read them though,
and think I'm mental.

Nothing
Is what it all comes down to.

# Hypermnesia

Meddling with the distant past,
I trespassed through those seldom moments
When my
"Love"
Might have wandered
Through your unwelcoming heart.
When you may have cultured
A few spontaneous feelings for me.
The rare moments when
My name might have provoked a smile
On your impassive yet beautiful face,
And my reflections might have
Made an appearance in your dreams.

Glancing through the book of memory,
I see that your name adorns its entirety.
Then I struck my conscious with questions,

How do I forget you?
Why does your image still shadow my heart?
Why does your name still rinse my soul in tears?

The answers may never be found,
There is a fact.
I have known all along…

Knowing you was a gift, irreplaceable.

Having you was a dream, irresistible.

And losing you was a curse, irreversible.

But I stumble upon those sacred moments,

Your memories make this painful journey
Seem all worthwhile.

# Love Locker

My first girlfriend
Had a box of things she liked to keep
Tucked under her bed, and stored away.

Mementos and keepsakes,
From past relationships.

At night when I can't sleep,
I wonder if you have a box to keep
Of all the things I've given/written/made for

You.

I wonder if you ever wish,
At night, when you're in bed,
That they were on your walls instead.

# Puzzled

Hope that it will go back together,
This puzzle that
Tumbled
And fell away.
Remember the picture that was once beheld,
Is now rubble, random, and strayed.

Smile and start to work forever.
Piecing together the fallen dead,
Toiling endlessly to fit these pieces,
Losing the picture inside your head.

Hope to stop it before it's lost forever,
Praying to just fade away.
The picture is gone and not returning,
But working constantly anyway.

Roll your eyes and sigh, disappointed;
Bang your head and lay down your woe.

Slam it,
Rip it,
Run in terror

Before the puzzle swallows you whole.
Pray you can piece it back together,

Hope that you can believe that lie.
The puzzle isn't fitting as it did before,
Stop, and sit, and laugh, and cry.

Rip it,
Slam it,
Start all over

Piece together what you can and will.
The picture is no longer remembered;

It has faded,
Giving my heart a chill.

# Canonized Clouds

Faces don't launch ships anymore,

They launch space shuttles.

Mine launches bottle rockets,

Flame splinters into smoke,

Becoming atmospheric.

I explode, now only vapor and debris,

Andyou go diving

To retrieve the bits of fuselage

For the model you're building

In your living room.

# TRL

You picked up my red lighter
You set it back down when you realized what
color it was.
You refused to use it,
But something sparked, nonetheless.
That was the moment I knew I'd fall in love
with you.

It may seem trivial, or mundane, but that's all it
took.

In a mere instant,
Just by being who you are,
You forever changed the way I see red lighters.
You gave them meaning,
Meaning I know I'll always associate with you.

You showed me in that brief window of time
That you were capable of changing everything,
Of giving all things a new, beautiful meaning.
You showed me how desperately I had been
aching for that,
For you.

You picked up my red lighter

And ignited the parts of my soul I swore would
never
Know warmth or light again.

You set it back down,
And didn't even realize that I was already
wrapped around your finger.
It was just a red lighter,
But it was enough to push me over the edge.

Free falling
With no parachute
And no fear of the impact ahead of me.

Falling, so safely.
Falling for you.
Falling with you.

And it was only a red lighter.

# Steep

The china teapot
Is chipped on the table,
Where we once had sat down to tea.

The water is cool,
And A fly in the air
Is my only guest,
Formally.

The fireplace where
I loved you is empty,
Without any wood left to burn.

And the blankets are frozen
By avalanches,
And winter that's come out of turn.

The pen that I write with
Is stiff and depraved,
And the sleep that I take is forbidden.

My darling, if only you'd followed,
"I love you"
With,
"Sweetheart, I'm only just kidding."

# Trust Fall Tumulus

Sometimes,
Love feels like bloodletting,
Sometimes A slow murder,
Like take everything until I have nothing left.

Take my breath away,
Make me beg for it,
And forget to give it back.

Sometimes a quick slash to the throat,
Like go for the jugular.
Tare it out with your teeth as you go in for that

Sweet kiss.

Make it feel like an act of intimacy, bring me to
my knees.

Make a mess, and walk away from it.

Like make your victim walk involuntarily,
Accept the blindfold, and cross their arms
behind their back.

Let them feel butterfly kisses on the nape of
their neck,

As you lean in to tie the rope.

Watch the sacrifice lie on the altar like it's a bed
of roses.
Watch them reach to feel petals but come away
With scarred fingers instead.

Like here,
Take my heart and promise not to crush it.

Like, let's play russian roulette
And pray that I can catch more than
L i e s
Between my teeth.

Like dig my grave,
And still give me hope
That you won't be the one
To push me into it.

# Blue Devil's Bedtime Story

An impatient hand
Picks up a pen and begins to write.

Minutes melt into hours,
A mind screaming it's thoughts
Out into the night's stillness--

Furious scribbling,
Agonized

Pauses.

In that bewitching hour,
I sat down to write you a letter.

My heart would not silence
It's anguished pleas,
And my mind would not
Cease it's reprimands.

Words were begging to
Fly from my fingertips.
So I took up a pen
And began to write.

No rhyme or reason to the words.

I realized that from these sleepless ramblings
Came a definite sense,
And the story of our lives emerged.

You were young and beautiful,
Wounded sensitive heart.
and I was just an incredulous girl,
Surprised by love.

It was bright and passionate
It whispered sweet forever's
In my yearning heart
And promised love eternal.

But as my story progressed,
My words grew dark and tragic
And I had to swallow my tears.

The story of old, how existence
Strangles love, chokes it to life.

And there was a trite metaphor
Of the great gulf that divided our souls.

How my mind began to betray me,
How I could not live with those
Murderous suspicions whispering within me.

"Is this what it means to grow apart?"

I quoted you meticulously
And shuttered with an unexpected sob.

How I wished to erase those bad years
That lingering destructive sadness
You despised in me so much…

How I longed to bring us back
To that innocence of new love
When you didn't hate me yet.

The letters became haggard.

The tone became tortured.

And the words began to wander.

As I wrote, I felt my heart
Bearing down within my chest.
I felt my mind unraveling.

The story then concluded,
Staggering lamely towards its end.
And the hands stopped moving;
The silence became oppressive.

Overwhelming.

The shadows
Grew darker in the room
And I sat,

My mind left without words,

My heart left without feeling.

# How Not To Cope

The only thing that I've learned from my
Mistakes,
Is how to cry so hard that my tears
Penetrate.
My skin and my breathing quickens,

I sob into silence as the universe spins on
Around me at full speed

In a blur of color.

My heart is broken into A thousand pieces,
The fractions cannot be put back together.

I push hard to get my space for breath,
So my heart is protected by a thick glass wall.

But I instead pushed too hard, into the blade of a
knife
And as my tears fall down, so does my grasp on
life.

Dependency on one figure,
The wrong one.

The busy streets packed with people

Glance toward me as I whisper my pain…
My years of screaming have dropped below their
radar.

Fingers string to walls and doors
As the weight of my head increases,
And my legs can't bear it.

My pain is increasing, growing tumors
And bursting the valves in my heart.

Waiting for an explosion, wishing--
So the world can see the pain I feel.

But I agonize over the intensity,
Until the only red I see
Are my eyes scratched out

When the evil of the world
Becomes too much to endure.

# Air In, Air Out.

I'm attracted to women
Who wear dresses and lipstick,
Heels and fake nails,
Fake lashes and fake hair,
But don't have a fake personality.

They look in the mirror more often than they
don't.

I'm attracted to women
Who are loud and creative,
Alcoholics, bold and generally mean,
But always sweet and caring towards me.

They usually love the color pink.

I'm attracted to women
Who do their own thing,
Have their own passions and hobbies,
Who talk about themselves incessantly.

They rarely ask me how I'm doing.

I'm attracted to women
Who make me laugh and cry,
Scream and talk and break my own heart,

They teach me to be a better person.

I'm attracted to women
Who push me out of my comfort zone,
Who make me go out,
And teach me new things.

They usually have a lesser intellect than me.

I'm attracted to women
Who are everything that I am not.

They cannot love my darkness as much as they
love my light.

# Heart Mark

A human only searching for a meaning,
A small little purpose,
But reality is too cruel,
The nights are too long,
My breaths, too painful,
No longer able to eat,
Trying to swallow,
But only choking;

Wanting to disappear,
Force it all down --

Pointless.

Sleepless nights
Are all that I am able to do.

Tossing and Turning

Trying to find a comfort that won't come,
Trying to not feel so alone.
The days have faded together
Like a muddy brown of colors.

I can't remember anything,
Blocking every emotion out of my head.

I can't even cry for relief,
Trying to fight back,
Trying to find my footing,
I only stumble back down.
I'm lost --

I've lost my voice –

I've lost what was once meaning.

# Adoration Hallucination

Emotions keep getting jumbled inside,
Words full of misconstrued definitions,
Argue with their own phrasing and crawl
Up and out
Of my mouth until they're all

S c a t t e r e d

Like marbles on the floor,
They pling and plop until settled
And wait for my eager hands
To arrange them into something cohesive--
A platter of answers to satiate my hungry soul
And as I swallow each

One. By. One.

The fleeting memory of freedom
From these confused voices drifts through the air
In scents of Rosemary and Thyme,
Simmering on the back burner,

Ready to Explode.

# Love Rhymes With Cardiac Arrest

Love is destruction, demolition.
When all supports are cast aside,
B l o w n   A p a r t
In the name of love.

When you collapse in a discarded heap,
The graceless toppled majesty
All rubble and luxurious agony,
Unable to rebuild the pillars of your identity
Without love.

When love breaks your bones with the sheer
weight of it
Upon your aching chest,

Love is dire, mortal wounds
That threaten to bleed the souls of itself.
In your clothing, your life,
That irrevocable stain.

Love is the wretchedness of so much violence
Compressed into one small human body.

Love is shackles, restraints.
Like that of prisoners, or of
Dangerous beasts.

And keeps you from feeling anything
Other than the leather chafing the skin,

The sensation of having no control,

The barbs penetrating the heart.

# When All Is Said and Done

I'm sitting with you
In a room full of

S i l e n c e

That is constantly being filled with
Things we refuse to say to one another.

I've left you with more of me
Than I ever intended to give.
I've felt more for you
Than my heart could ever afford.

I've come back to ask for absolutely nothing in
return.

I thought I had nothing left to say to you;
I swore that you were never really listening,
anyway.

But if you did so much as ask me for one last
reminder --
You should know that my days have always
begun and ended

With you.

One way or another,
Whether you were actually here
Or nowhere to be found.

The nerves inside of my body that refuse to feel
any more,
Still remember your touch.

The rest that have the audacity to feel anything,
Still ache for you.

My paralyzed heart still dances
When I hear your voice
-I never hear your voice any more-

My bittersweet memory
Still thinks you taste like honey.

My hands will never
Outgrow you.

And my mind could never unlearn you.

So, if you did so much as ask me for one last
reminder --

You should know,


That it will always end with you.

www.ingramcontent.com/pod-product-compliance
Lightning Source LLC
Chambersburg PA
CBHW060917130726
48001CB00006B/2276